CHRISTOPHER FRY

The Boy with a Cart

CUTHMAN, SAINT OF SUSSEX

A Play

FREDERICK MULLER LTD.
LONDON

THIS SECOND EDITION PUBLISHED BY
FREDERICK MULLER LTD.
IN 1945
PRINTED IN GREAT BRITAIN
BY BUTLER & TANNER LTD.
FROME & LONDON

Tenth Impression 1953

THIS BOOK WAS ORIGINALLY PUBLISHED IN
1939 BY OXFORD UNIVERSITY PRESS

THE BOY WITH A CART

★

CHARACTERS

(In order of appearance)

CUTHMAN
BESS AND MILDRED } *Cornish Neighbours*
MATT AND TIB
CUTHMAN'S MOTHER

TAWM
HIS DAUGHTER
HIS SON-IN-LAW
A FARMER   } *Villagers of Steyning*
MRS. FIPPS
ALFRED AND
DEMIWULF, HER SONS

Cornish neighbours, Mowers, Villagers of Steyning, and The People of South England.

THE BOY WITH A CART

THE PEOPLE OF SOUTH ENGLAND :
In our fields, fallow and burdened, in grass and furrow,
In barn and stable, with scythe, flail, or harrow,
Sheepshearing, milking or mowing, on labour that's older
Than knowledge, with God we work shoulder to shoulder ;
God providing, we dividing, sowing, and pruning ;
Not knowing yet and yet sometimes discerning :
Discerning a little at Spring when the bud and shoot
With pointing finger show the hand at the root,
With stretching finger point the mood in the sky :
Sky and root in joint action ; and the cry
Of the unsteady lamb allying with the brief
Sunlight, with the curled and cautious leaf.

> Coming out from our doorways on April evenings
> When to-morrow's sky is written on the slates
> We have discerned a little, we have learned
> More than the gossip that comes to us over our gates.
> We have seen old men cracking their memories for dry
>   milk.
> We have seen old women dandling shadows ;
> But coming out from our doorways, we have felt
> Heaven ride with Spring into the meadows.

We have felt the joint action of root and sky, of man
And God, when day first risks the hills, and when
The darkness hangs the hatchet in the barn
And scrapes the heavy boot against the iron :
In first and last twilight, before wheels have turned
Or after they are still, we have discerned :
Guessed at divinity working above the wind,
Working under our feet; or at the end
Of a furrow, watching the lark dissolve in sun,
We have almost known, a little have known

I

The work that is with our work, as we have seen
The blackthorn hang where the Milky Way has been :
Flower and star spattering the sky
And the root touched by some divinity.

> Coming out from our doorways on October nights
> We have seen the sky unfreeze and a star drip
> Into the south : experienced alteration
> Beyond experience. We have felt the grip
> Of the hand on earth and sky in careful coupling
> Despite the jibbing, man destroying, denying,
> Disputing, or the late frost looting the land
> Of green. Despite flood and the lightning's rifle
> In root and sky we can discern the hand.

It is there in the story of Cuthman, the working together
Of man and God like root and sky ; the son
Of a Cornish shepherd, Cuthman, the boy with a cart,
The boy we saw trudging the sheep-tracks with his mother
Mile upon mile over five counties ; one
Fixed purpose biting his heels and lifting his heart.
We saw him ; we saw him with a grass in his mouth,
  chewing
And travelling. We saw him building at last
A church among whortleberries. And you shall see
Now, in this place, the story of his going
And his building.—A thousand years in the past
There was a shepherd, and his son had three
Sorrows come together on him. Shadow
The boy. Follow him now as he runs in the meadow.

[*Enter* CUTHMAN, *running. He stops short as he sees* TWO
NEIGHBOURS *approaching.*

CUTHMAN : Now, my legs, look what a bad place
  You've brought me into : Bess and Mildred coming :
  Two nice neighbours with long noses. Now
  I should like the sun to go down, and I could close
  As the daisy closes : put up my shutters, slap,

2

Here in the long grass. Whip the world away
In one collapsing gesture. And you can't
Waken a sleeping daisy with a shaking.—
Well, green is green and flesh is a different matter.
Green is under their feet, but my lot's better.
I can say to them Neighbours, believe it or not,
God is looking after my father's sheep.
But the simple truth is harder to tell than a lie.
The trouble I'll have, and the trouble they'll have to
    believe it !
And I wasn't looking for trouble this bright morning.

   [*As the* NEIGHBOURS *come up to him :*

Good-morning, good-morning !

BESS : Good-morning, Cuthman.

CUTHMAN : This is the morning to take the air, flute-clear
And, like a lutanist, with a hand of wind
Playing the responsive hills, till a long vibration
Spills across the fields, and the chancelled larches
Sing like Lenten choirboys, a green treble ;
Playing at last the skylark into rising,
The wintered cuckoo to a bashful stutter.
It is the first day of the year that I've king'd
Myself on the rock, sat myself in the wind :
It was laying my face on gold. And when I stood
I felt the webs of winter all blow by
And in the bone-dry runnel of the earth
Spring restart her flood.

MILDRED :   We came to find you,
Cuthman, expecting to find you with the sheep.

CUTHMAN : Dinner-time is passed, and my father
Has forgotten where his son chews on a grass
And thinks of meat.

BESS :   Cuthman-chick, your father——

CUTHMAN : I know what you will say to me : My father
Has my promise to be shepherd till he send

Another boy to take my place and tend them.
And, promise-bound, what do I do careering
Like a stone down a hill, like a holidaymaker
With only his own will ? But they're safe,
Those little sheep, more than with me beside them,
More than with twenty Cuthmans now God minds them.

BESS : Cuthman-boy——

CUTHMAN :   It is so ! Not to-day
Only, but other days God took the crook
And watched them in the wind. One other day
My father let the time go by, forgetting
To send away the herdboy to relieve me.
However often I stood up on the rock
Shouting "Here's Cuthman ! Here's a hungry shepherd !"
My only relief came from the clouds that closed
With the sun and dodged again : the sun that tacked
From dinner-time into the afternoon.
I was as empty as a vacant barn.
It might have been because my stomach was empty
That I was suddenly filled up with faith—
Suddenly parcelled with faith like a little wain
In a good hay-season and, all round, the hills
Lay at my feet like collies. So I took
My crook, and round the sheep I drew a circle
Saying " God guard them here, if God will guard them " ;
Drew it, though as a fence I knew it was less
Good than a bubble. Then to yearling and ewe
And lamb I said " Give no trouble " ; laid
My crook against the rock and went to dinner.
When I came back no lamb or yearling or ewe
Had broken through. They gently lay together
Cropping the crook's limited pasture, though
The unhedged green said " Trespass."—This is true.
Come, and I'll show you. I have waited again
To go to dinner and father has forgotten——

BESS : Cuthman, your father is dead.

4

MILDRED :　　　　　　　　　　We came to tell you.

CUTHMAN : You can't say that to me. I was speaking the truth.

MILDRED : We were speaking the truth.

CUTHMAN :　　　　　　　　　You came to make me sorry,
But you're breaking the sun over your knees to say
My father's dead. My father is strong and well.
Each morning my father buckles himself to,
Like a leather strap, and at night comes to the fire
His hands bare with well-water to tell
The story of Jesus. So he will talk to-night,
Clenching his hands against Gethsemane,
Opening his hands to feel the Ascension
As though after dry weeks he were feeling
The first rain. Every evening I have watched,
And his face was like a live coal under the smoking
Shadows on the ceiling.

BESS :　　　　　　　　What can we do,
Cuthman, if you're unbelieving ?

MILDRED :　　　　　　　　Come
Down with us and see him.

CUTHMAN :　　　　　　Let me alone.
No ; if I come you'll take me to a place
Where truth will laugh and scatter like a magpie.
Up here, my father waits for me at home
And God sits with the sheep.

BESS :　　　　　　　　Cuthman, you make it
Hard for us to tell you.

MILDRED :　　　　　　The trouble we have
To tell him, and the trouble he has to believe.

BESS : How can we help you, Cuthman, in your trouble
If our words go by like water in a sieve ?

CUTHMAN : Let me alone.

5

MILDRED : It's funny the way it takes him.
I don't even know if he really understands.
I don't even know if he really thinks we're lying.

BESS : Well, I don't know. Perhaps he feels like crying
And that's why he wants us to go.

MILDRED : It may be so.

BESS (*to* CUTHMAN) : If we can be any help——

MILDRED : If there's anything we can do——

BESS : We'd better go to his mother again, poor soul,
And get her a bite or two. She's certain not
To eat a thing unless somebody's by.

MILDRED : It's a merciful thing she had the sense to cry.

[*They go away down the hill.*

CUTHMAN : What have I done ? Did I steal God away
From my father to guard my sheep ? How can I keep
Pace with a pain that comes in my head so fast ?
How did I make the day brittle to break ?
What sin brought in the strain, the ominous knock,
The gaping seam ? Was it a boast on the rock,
The garrulous game ? What have I done to him ?
Father, if you are standing by to help me—
Help me to cry.

[*He falls on to the ground.*

THE PEOPLE OF SOUTH ENGLAND :
The day is pulled up by the root and dries,
    And the sun drains to the hollow sea.
        Heaven is quarried with cries.
        Song dies on the tree.

The thongs of the daylight are drawn and slack.
    The dew crawls down to earth like tears.
        Root and sky break
        And will not mend with prayers.

6

Only the minutes fall and stack
  Like a rising drum
    Where, thin as a draught through the crack,
      Death has whistled home.

CUTHMAN (*rising to his knees*) : I have ears stopped with earth
Not to have heard the door-catch as he went,
The raven gulping dew, the crow on the stack,
Nor grasped the warning of the howling dog
To bring me to my feet, to have me home ;
Heard soon enough to run and still to find him ;
For me to say " You have been a father
Not to lie down so soon, not to forget
Till I forget the last hand that shall hold me."
Still to be able to find him, and to see
How he put down his cup and dried his mouth
And turned as heaven shut behind him.

THE PEOPLE OF SOUTH ENGLAND :
      How is your faith now, Cuthman ?
      Your faith that the warm world hatched,
      That spread its unaccustomed colour
      Up on the rock, game and detached ?

      You see how sorrow rises, Cuthman,
      How sorrow rises like the heat
      Even up to the plumed hills
      And the quickest feet.

      Pain is low against the ground
      And grows like a weed.
      Is God still in the air
      And in the seed ?

      Is God still in the air
      Now that the sun is down ?
      They are afraid in the city,
      Sleepless in the town,

Cold on the roads,
Desperate by the river.
Can faith for long elude
Prevailing fever ?

CUTHMAN : I have stayed too long with the children, a boy
    sliding
On the easy ice, skating the foolish silver
Over the entangling weed and the eddying water.
If I have only ventured the reflection
And not the substance, and accepted only
A brushwork sun skidding ahead of me
And not the dealer of days and docker of time ;
Only the blue-print of a star and not
The star ; accepted only the light's boundary
To the shadow and not the shadow, only the gloss
And burnish of the leaf and not the leaf—
Let me see now with truer sight, O God
Of root and sky ; let me at last be faithful
In perception, and in action that is born
Of perception, even as I have been faithful
In the green recklessness of little knowledge.
Grant this, O God, that I may grow to my father
As he grew to Thy Son, and be his son
Now and for always.

VOICES OF NEIGHBOURS : Cuthman ! Cuthman ! Cuth-
    man !

CUTHMAN : Here's the valley breaking against the hill.

PEOPLE OF ENGLAND : Sorrow rises like the heat.

CUTHMAN : No longer dryshod can I keep my will.

PEOPLE OF ENGLAND : Nor the plumed feet.

CUTHMAN : The circle is broken and the sheep wander.
They pull the branches of the myrtle under :
Nibble the shadow of the cypress, trample
The yew, and break the willow of its tears.
This is no grief of theirs.

8

[Two Neighbours, Matt *and* Tib, *come up to him.*

MATT :   Cuthman, your father
  Is dead.

CUTHMAN : They told me.

TIB :   Your mother is sick.

CUTHMAN :   She is grieving.

MATT : She is calling for you. We heard her voice through
  the window.

CUTHMAN : I shall come soon. But the sheep are foot-loose
    and green-
  Hungry. They will be lost in sundown, and no
  Bell-wether. Where would my mother tell me to go,
  To her or bring them home ?

TIB :   You have no home,
  Cuthman.

CUTHMAN : I have no father, but my mother
  Is at home.

MATT :   Your home is sold over your head.
  There's no roof over your sorrow : nor a patch
  Of ground to know your name in ; nothing, son,
  Nothing in the valley.

CUTHMAN :   My mother's at home.

TIB : Your mother is sick. What will you do, Cuthman ?

CUTHMAN : I will drive my father's sheep home to my
  mother.

  [*Exit* CUTHMAN.

MATT : Could we have told him the rest of it : the last
  Of the rotten business ?

TIB :   I had said enough.
  I had done more damage with words than downpour
  Did the crops. Look how his wing is dragging.

MATT : Look what he still has to know. His father dead,
  The house sold over his head, and still the blow,
  The final straw : no money in the house,
  Not a flip of silver he can toss,
  And double in his hand.

TIB :   But still we said
  Enough. And what we said he scarcely knows.
  He carries the first trouble, and the rest
  Only dog at his heels.

MATT :   Make your way down.
  None of us knows the way a neighbour feels.

  [*Exeunt.*

THE PEOPLE OF SOUTH ENGLAND :
  Out of this, out of the first incision
  Of mortality on mortality, there comes
  The genuflexion, and the partition of pain
  Between man and God ; there grows the mutual action,
  The perspective to the vision.

  Out of this, out of the dereliction
  Of a mild morning, comes the morning's motive,
  The first conception, the fusion of root and sky ;
  Grows the achievement of the falling shadow,
  Pain's patient benediction.

NEIGHBOURS (*entering*) :
  One after the other we have gone to the boy,
  Offering him advice, condolences, and recommendations
  To relations in more well-to-do places.
  We have offered him two good meals a day.—
  My wife is a bad cook but she gives large helpings.—
  We have done what we could ; we can't do more.
  But he goes his own way. All that we say
  He seems to ignore. He keeps himself apart,
  Speaking only out of politeness,
  Eating out his heart, and of all things on earth
  He is making a cart !

10

One after the other we have gone to him and said,
" Cuthman, what use will a cart be to you ? "
He scarcely so much as raised his head, only
Shook it, saying, " I will tell you some other time ;
I am in a hurry."

One after the other we have gone also
To his mother, offering advice, condolences,
Recommendations to our distant relations.
His poor mother, she suffers a great deal in her legs.
And we have said to her, " We hope you will excuse
Our asking, we hope you will not think us
Inquisitive, but what is your boy Cuthman
So busy on ? "—And she replied each time :
" It is something after his own heart."

We are none the wiser : and after all
It is none of our business, though it's only natural
We should take a certain amount of interest.

One after the other we have gone indoors
Turning it over in our minds as we went
About our chores. What will the old woman do,
Dear heart, with no roof over her head, no man,
No money, and her boy doing nothing
But make a cart ?

" I will tell you some other time," he said.
" I am in a hurry." Well, that's his look-out.
It's not for us to worry.

   [*They go back to the village.*

   [*Enter* CUTHMAN *with a cart, and his* MOTHER.

CUTHMAN : If you turn round, Mother, you can see the village almost under your feet. You won't get another view.
It's sinking like a ship. We're looking at the last of it.

MOTHER : My legs, my legs ! That hill's finished them. I
should have stopped at the bottom. Your grandmother

used to say to me when I was a girl : " Daughter," she would say, " never get above yourself. It will be your downfall." Little did she guess what things would happen to me, and it's just as well. I was her favourite daughter.

CUTHMAN : We shall never see it again ; we shall never look again at the sun on the white walls, my swaddling-clothes put out to dry. I am out of them once and for all.

MOTHER : What on earth are you doing talking about your swaddling clothes ? I wish I knew what was the matter with you. You were shortened at five months. You were walking at a year. . . . Dear heart, I don't know how ever I got up as far as I have.

CUTHMAN : I have never known anything except the village and these few hills. I have two eyes, but how can I know if I have a memory for faces ? I have two legs, but they've only carried me backwards and forwards like an old flight of steps. All my life I have been on a tether, but now I have slipped it and the world is green from side to side.

MOTHER : You know nothing of the world, Cuthman, and I'm thankful to say it. I am an old woman and I know too much. I have seen it. I've seen too much of it. Before I married your father I worked as a laundress at Letherwithel. That's fourteen miles away. And after we were married he brought me here, fourteen miles sitting behind him on a horse.

CUTHMAN : But now you're going to travel in style ; we've got a cart for you to ride in.

MOTHER (*looking at the cart and back at* CUTHMAN) : Sometimes I think you can't be very well, Cuthman. . . . Your father and I first met one October. He had ridden over to the fair and it came on to rain.

CUTHMAN : We have more than fourteen miles to go. Last night I looked up and saw the full moon standing behind a tree. It was like a strange man walking into the room at night without knocking. It made my heart jump. . . . I don't know how many miles we'll have to go.

MOTHER : Cuthman! Look your mother in the face. What are you going to do with her?

CUTHMAN : We're going to travel.

MOTHER : I wish I knew what to do with you. The trouble is, you don't give me time to speak. You rush me up a hill so that I lose all my breath. You won't listen to reason. Where are you taking me? I insist upon knowing—don't think you can get away with those mysterious wags of your head. I shan't take another step until I know.

CUTHMAN : We're going to see the world, Mother.

MOTHER : I'm an old woman and I won't be joked to. Who gave you this man's address?

CUTHMAN : I haven't got an address, Mother.

MOTHER : I'm going to be very ill. (*She sits on the cart.*)

CUTHMAN : We shall find our way in the world, Mother, and I've made you a cart. You can rest as you go.

MOTHER : I've always stood up for you to the neighbours. They have come to me often enough and said : " Cuthman isn't practical ; he's going to find life very difficult." And I have always said to them : " Never you mind. Cuthman's my son, and when I was a girl his grandmother used to say to me, ' Daughter, whatever else you may be, you have your wits.' "—And in the end, after all the trouble I've had to bring you up, you want to use me like a barrowful of turnips.

CUTHMAN : Mother, can you remember the neighbours' faces when you came into the village riding on the back of my father's horse?

MOTHER : The neighbours' faces? I should think so indeed, like yesterday. They were all stuck out of the windows and they were shouting out to each other, " What do you think of that? He's gone out of his way to find something! "

13

They liked the look of me at once, they told me afterwards. We have always been very respected in the village.

CUTHMAN : That's just it ; so it wouldn't do at all to end your days as a beggar in the place where you've always been respected ; it wouldn't do to end them in a little hovel that some one would let us have, in a corner of one of their sheds, living on their left-overs and perhaps a good meal at Christmas.

MOTHER : This is the finish of me, I can't survive it. There wasn't a day in the week that I didn't have a clean apron. And now there's no one to look after me except a fool of a son, and he wants to trundle me all over the world like a load of fish.

CUTHMAN : What do you think I have been doing, Mother, while I sat all day on the doorstep, working at the cart ? You couldn't get a whistle or a word out of me. But I've been thinking and praying ; and wherever we go, if we go wisely and faithfully, God will look after us. Calamity is the forking of the roads, and when we have gone a little way up the turn we shall find it equally green. We have nibbled the old pasture bare, and now we must look for longer grass.

MOTHER : I'm too old for it, too old for it. The world's no greener than a crab in the sea, and I don't like its nip. . . . Oh, what a disaster ! What a wealth of affliction ! Nothing between me and the weather except my second-best bombasin !

CUTHMAN : You'll see ; after a bit, and after a bit of worry perhaps, we shall come into our own again. You'll find yourself saying, " This is just the place for us ; just what we wanted." And there'll be work for me to do. I shall buckle myself to every morning, and you shall have a white apron. These last days, while I sat on the step, I prayed. I was praying while I worked at the cart.

MOTHER : That's the best thing ; it's always the best thing.

I have been praying too. But I'm an old woman and I know the dangers. The world's a bothering place, that's what I can't make you see : the world isn't Heaven and I know it well.

CUTHMAN : But the world has more than one hill and valley and that's the comfort of it. Get easy, Mother ; we're leaving.

MOTHER : I'm sick at the thought of it. Your grandmother would cry herself into her grave if she were alive to see us.

CUTHMAN : But as it is nobody is crying. (*He turns and looks for the last time at the village.*)

MOTHER (*as they go*) : It is just as well that we went away respected ; that will be something to remember at any rate. I told the villagers, " We are going away ; Cuthman has found work to do."

CUTHMAN : And hard work, too, Mother, if there are many hills. You're no feather.

[*They set off on their journey, the* MOTHER *in the cart, and a rope round* CUTHMAN's *neck attached to the handles. As they go* CUTHMAN *begins to whistle. They are heard going away into the distance.*

THE PEOPLE OF SOUTH ENGLAND :
Stone over stone, over the shaking track,
They start their journey : jarring muscle and aching
Back crunch the fading county into
Dust. Stone over stone, over the trundling
Mile, they stumble and trudge : where the thirsty bramble
Begs at the sleeve, the pot-hole tugs the foot.
Stone over stone, over the trampled sunlight,
Over the flagging day, over the burn
And blister of the dry boot, they flog their way
To where the journeyless and roofless trees
Muster against the plunging of the dark :
Where the shut door and the ministering fire
Have shrunk across the fields to a dog's bark,

To a charred circle in the grass.
No floorboard mouse, no tattling friend ; only
The flickering bat dodging the night air,
Only the stoat clapping the fern as it runs.

Stone over stone, Cuthman has spoken out
His faith to his mother. She has been comforted
A little ; begins to believe in her son.
He has made her clumsy rhymes to laugh at.
She has tried to tell him stories of his grandmother,
But it is hard to talk buffeted by a cart.

After these miles, at last when the day leans
On the wall, at last when the vagrant hour flops
In the shade, they found a protected place, a ground
Where limbs and prayers could stretch between root and.
Root, between root and sky ; and they slept under curfew
Or Cuthman slept. His mother was chasing fears
Until daylight. " What is rustling in the grass ?
What shakes in the tree ? What is hiding in
The shadow ? " And Cuthman said, " God is there.
God is waiting with us."

Stone over stone, in the thin morning, they plod
Again, until they come to a field where mowers
Sweep their scythes under the dry sun.

[*The* MOWERS *at work in the field. They sing.*

MOWERS : The muscle and the meadow
              Make men sing,
          And the grass grows high
          Like lashes to a lady's eye.
          Sickle-blades go sliding by
              And so does everything,
          Grass, the year, and a merry friend
              All at last come to an end.

[*Enter* CUTHMAN *wheeling his* MOTHER. *The* MOWERS *stop
work and nudge each other.*

16

MOTHER : I have gone up and down stairs fifty times a day when you were a baby and your aunt lived with us. She was an invalid but you wouldn't remember her. I have dug in the garden for your father, and had all the house-work to do into the bargain. You don't know the work there is to do in a house. Your father's brother came to see us (you were only two months old at the time) and he said : " Sister, you must be made of rope. My wife has help in the house, but nevertheless when she takes a broom in her hand she bursts into tears." And I wasn't young, you must remember. I was nearly forty years old when I married your father. But never mind that. The point is that we've come a long way, so far that it's a wonder we've still kept the sun in sight ; and I've been so jogged and jerked that I think your uncle must have been right. I begin to think that I'm really made of rope.

[*At this moment the rope round* CUTHMAN'S *shoulders breaks, and his mother is rolled on to the ground. The* MOWERS *burst out laughing.*

CUTHMAN : Are you hurt, Mother ? The rope broke. How are you, Mother, are you all right ?

MOTHER : Oh ! Oh ! If your mother ever walks again you'll be luckier than you deserve. This is what it has come to. You bring me all these miles to throw me on the ground.

CUTHMAN : The rope broke, Mother. Are you hurt ?

MOTHER : Of course I'm hurt. I'm more than hurt, I'm injured.

CUTHMAN : Let me help you up ; see if you can walk.

MOTHER : Walk ? I might as well try to fly. What are all those people laughing at ?

CUTHMAN : Try to stand on your legs.

MOTHER : They're laughing at me ; that's what's the matter with them. They're laughing at an old woman who has had a misfortune. I told you what kind of place the world was, Cuthman, and I shall put a stop to it. I tell you, I've a sense of humour, but I won't be laughed at. (*She gets to her feet and rounds on the* MOWERS.) I don't know who you are, but I'm glad I wasn't born in your part of the country. Where I was born we knew how to behave ; we knew better than to laugh at an old woman who had come to grief We were very respected in the village where we come from, I may tell you ; but as it happens we decided to travel. (*The* MOWERS *give an even louder roar of laughter.*) All right, all right ! One of these days you'll laugh for too long, you'll laugh yourselves into trouble, take my word for it.

CUTHMAN : I must make a new rope for the cart ; I shall have to make it out of withies. We shall find some at the stream we just passed over, remember, Mother ? Fifty yards back or so. What will you do ? Would you rather stay here, or will you come with me ?

1ST MOWER : Did you hear what the boy said ? A rope cf withies ! What a joke !

2ND MOWER : Don't you go and make the rope too strong, baby boy. You needn't go farther than the end of the earth to find a fortune !

[*They go off again into a roar of laughter.*

MOTHER : I should like to box the ears of the whole lot, but there are too many of them ; it would take too long.

CUTHMAN : Let's go, Mother ; let's find the withies.

MOTHER : I may be lame, but I'd walk away from this place if it was the last thing I did.

[*They go off,* CUTHMAN *wheeling the cart.*

3RD MOWER (*singing after them*) :
> Don't fall into the stream, Mother.
> The water's very high.
> We might not hear you scream, Mother.
> And we'd hate to see you die !

[*They laugh again, and sing it all together.*

4TH MOWER : Here, did you feel that ? A drop of rain !

1ST MOWER : Never ; never on your life.

4TH MOWER : I swear it was. I felt a drop of rain. Look at the clouds coming up.

2ND MOWER : He's right. I felt a drop on my hand, and another, and another !

3RD MOWER : Don't stand about then. For the crop's sake, get at the hay !

[*They feverishly set to work.*

1ST MOWER : It's no good. We can do nothing at all—the whole sky is opening.

THE PEOPLE OF SOUTH ENGLAND :

That is rain on dry ground. We heard it :
We saw the little tempest in the grass,
The panic of anticipation : heard
The uneasy leaves flutter, the air pass
In a wave, the fluster of the vegetation ;

Heard the first spatter of drops, the outriders
Larruping on the road, hitting against
The gate of the drought, and shattering
On to the lances of the tottering meadow.
It is rain ; it is rain on dry ground,

Rain riding suddenly out of the air,
Battering the bare walls of the sun.
It is falling on to the tongue of the blackbird,
Into the heart of the thrush ; the dazed valley
Sings it down. Rain, rain on dry ground !

This is the urgent decision of the day,
The urgent drubbing of earth, the urgent raid
On the dust ; downpour over the flaring poppy,
Deluge on the face of noon, the flagellant
Rain drenching across the air.—The day

19

Flows in the ditch ; bubble and twisting twig
And the sodden morning swirl along together
Under the crying hedge. And where the sun
Ran on the scythes, the rain runs down
The obliterated field, the blunted crop.

[*The* MOWERS *have fled from the rain, leaving the hay to
disaster.*

THE PEOPLE OF SOUTH ENGLAND :
> The rain stops.
> The air is sprung with green.
> The intercepted drops
> Fall at their leisure ; and between
> The threading runnels on the slopes
> The snail drags his caution into the sun.

[*Re-enter* CUTHMAN *and his* MOTHER, *his rope of withies
fastened from the cart to his shoulder.*

CUTHMAN : All the mowers are gone.

MOTHER : If I'd been the ground under their feet I should
have swallowed the lot.

CUTHMAN : But look at the field ! You might think the sky
had crashed on to it.

MOTHER : Rain ! I never !

CUTHMAN : Down by the stream there wasn't even a
shower ; we had a hard job keeping the sun out of our eyes.
But here the crop is ruined and everywhere is running with
water. Only a field away, and we felt nothing of it !

MOTHER : They were laughing at an old woman come to
grief. I told them how it would be. You'll go on laughing
too long, I said. And look what a plight they're in now.—
Poor souls.

CUTHMAN : Mother——

MOTHER : What is it, son ?

CUTHMAN : When the withies break——

MOTHER : What ! When the withies break ! Do you think I'll get back into that cart when I shall be expecting every bump to be my last ? You don't know your mother, Cuthman. She doesn't walk up to misfortune like a horse to sugar.

CUTHMAN : I shall be ready for it this time, Mother.

MOTHER : So you will, and so shall I. My eyes will be round your neck every minute of the day.

CUTHMAN : I shall look out and keep a good hold on the handles. And when the withies break——

MOTHER : If you can tell me what happens then it will be a relief to me.

CUTHMAN : We won't go any farther.

MOTHER : That's just what I was afraid of. All my bones will be broken to smithereens.

CUTHMAN : When we had gone down to the bank of the stream
And were cutting willow-shoots (listen, Mother,
This is something I must tell you : how
From to-day for all my days life has to be,
How life is proving) while the rain was falling
Behind us in the field though we still wore
The sun like a coat, I felt the mood
Of the meadow change, as though a tide
Had turned in the sap, or heaven from the balance
Of creation had shifted a degree.
The skirling water crept into a flow,
The sapling flickered in my hand, timber
And flesh seemed of equal and old significance.
At that place and then, I tell you, Mother,
God rode up my spirit and drew in
Beside me. His breath met on my breath, moved
And mingled. I was taller then than death.
Under the willows I was taller than death.

MOTHER : I saw you standing quiet. I said to myself
He has something in his heart, he has something
That occupies him.

CUTHMAN :   We shall go as far
As the withies take us. There, where they break,
Where God breaks them, you shall set up
House again and put clean paper on
Larder shelves. And there where God breaks them
And scoops our peace out of a strange field
I shall build my answer in plank and brick,
Labour out my thanks in plaster and beam
And stone. You, Mother, and I, when God
Brings our settled days again, will build
A church where the withies are broken, a church to pray
   in
When you have put your broom away, and untied
Your apron.

MOTHER :   Build a church, with our own hands ?

CUTHMAN : With our own hands, Mother, and with our
   own
Love of God and with nothing else ; for I have
Nothing else ; I have no craft or knowledge of joint
Or strain, more than will make a cart, and even
The cart you scarcely would call handsome. What
Did I learn to do after I found my feet
And found my tongue ? Only to seem as intelligent
As the neighbours' children whatever happened ; to be
Always a little less than myself in order
To avoid being conspicuous. But now
I am less than I would be, less
Than I must be ; my buzzing life is less
Than my birth was or my death will be. The church
And I shall be built together ; and together
Find our significance. Breaking and building
In the progression of this world go hand in hand.
And where the withies break I shall build.

MOTHER : I am always lagging a little behind your thoughts,
  I am always put out of breath by them. No doubt
  I shall arrive one of these days.

CUTHMAN :   In, Mother.
  We shall arrive together if the cart holds good.

MOTHER : It always seems to me I take my life
  In my hands, every time I get into this
  Contraption.

CUTHMAN :   Listen to that ! A hard week's work
  And she calls it a contraption !

  [*They set out again.*

THE PEOPLE OF SOUTH ENGLAND :
        For the lifetime of a sapling-rope
        Plaited in the eye of God,
        Among the unfamiliar twine
        Of England, he still must strain
        And plug the uneasy slope,
        And struggle in heavy sun, and plod
        Out his vision ; still must haunt
        Along the evening battlement
        Of hills and creep in the long valleys
        In the insect's trail, the small the dogged
        Pinhead of dust, by whose desire
        A church shall struggle into the air.
        No flattering builder of follies
        Would lay foundations so deep and rugged.
        A church, a church will branch at last
        Above a country pentecost,
        And the vision at last will find its people
        And the prayers at last be said.
        This is how he mutters and how
        Weariness runs off his brow.
        Already the bell climbs in the steeple,
        The belfrey of his shaggy head,
        And the choir over and over again
        Sings in the chancel of his brain.

Across the shorn downs, to the foot,
To Steyning, the last laborious track
Is trapesed and the withies at his neck
Untwist and break.
So he tips the stone from his boot,
Laughs at the smoking stack,
At the carthorse shaking its brass,
And knows the evening will turn a friendly face.

[*Enter* TAWM, *an old man. He keeps a look-out over his shoulder.*

TAWM : They'll be after me again, not a corner of Steyning
but they'll ferret me out ; my daughter and my daughter's
husband and my daughter's daughter ; my nephew and
my nephew's nephews : they'll be after me. " There's a
cold wind, Father (or uncle or grandfather or whatever it
is) ; take care of yourself, wrap yourself up ; it's going to
rain, it's likely to snow, there's a heavy dew. What do they
think I was born into this world for if it wasn't to die of it ? "

VOICES (*off stage*) : Father ! Father !

TAWM : The ferrets, the ferrets ! If I climbed up on to a
cloud they'd find me out and bring me my hat.

[*Enter his* DAUGHTER *and his* SON-IN-LAW.

DAUGHTER : Father, whatever are you thinking about ?
Why ever do you want to go walking about the fields with
a cold wind blowing ? I've got your supper waiting for you.

SON-IN-LAW : Here's your hat.

TAWM (*with bitterness*) : Daughter, your husband's a most
obliging man. He brings me my hat when the wind's in
my hair. Thank you, son ; you're an invaluable fellow.

[*Enter* CUTHMAN *wheeling his* MOTHER.

DAUGHTER : Who ever have we got here ? (*She giggles.*)

SON-IN-LAW : They're nobody I know. I've seen everybody
twenty miles around and this is none of them.

24

TAWM : They're strangers, likely as not. If I was challenged I shouldn't be afraid to say that these are strangers.

DAUGHTER : What does he think he's doing going around like that with the old woman ? I've never seen anything like it. (*She giggles again.*)

TAWM : You've got no understanding of geography, daughter. All the places in the world have their own ways and this young man is doing so because it's his way.

MOTHER : Cuthman, this is a very pretty place, quite a picture. The beauties of nature always make me feel honest with myself.

CUTHMAN : Mother, the withies have broken !

MOTHER : I remember when I was a girl I went up to my mother with a bunch of cornflowers in my hand——

CUTHMAN : Mother, the withies ! The withies have broken !

MOTHER : Nothing has happened to me ; I'm still where I was ; I'm still in the cart.

CUTHMAN : I was holding it firm ; but look at them, they've chafed in two. You can get out of it now, Mother ; we're not going any farther.

MOTHER : If ever I sit in a chair again I shan't recognize myself. What a very pretty place ! Are we really stopping here, Cuthman ?

CUTHMAN : Yes, Mother ; we've arrived.

MOTHER : It's too much to believe all in a minute. But one thing's quite certain : it'll be a good many nights before I stop bumping about in my dreams.

[*A crowd of* VILLAGERS *has collected. They stare at* CUTH-MAN *and his* MOTHER.

CUTHMAN : Why do you think all these people are staring, Mother ?

MOTHER : They're welcoming us. It's like old times. It was just like this when your father brought me home on the back of his horse.

CUTHMAN (*calling out to them*) : Could you tell me the name of this place, please ?

[*The* VILLAGERS *continue to stare.*

CUTHMAN : I say ! Would you mind telling us where we are ?—They're dumb, Mother.

MOTHER : They like us and respect us. One of these days they'll tell us so. It was just like this when your father brought me home, and they told me afterwards they liked the look of me at once they said.

TAWM : Good-evening.

CUTHMAN : Good-evening.

MOTHER : Good-evening.

TAWM : Can I be of any help to you at all ?

CUTHMAN : Perhaps you could tell us the name of this place.

TAWM : P'r'aps I could. I've lived here seventy years, so p'r'aps I could. It's Steyning, if I remember right.

CUTHMAN : Steyning. . . . The church at Steyning.

TAWM : The church ? If that's what you're after you've got the wrong place ; there's no church here.

A WOMAN : This is a poor place and we're poor people ; we must pray on the bare ground.

CUTHMAN : I've come to build a church.

[*This causes a sensation among the* VILLAGERS.

MOTHER : It's an idea that my boy has ; he has got it very much at heart. But I don't know what we can be looking like ; I can't imagine at all. You must take us for tramps. Before my husband died I always hoped that one day we'd see the country together, but it really is very tiring. Some one ought to do something about the state of the roads. My husband was a farmer

26

TAWM : Does the boy want work to do ?

CUTHMAN : Yes, I do.

TAWM : How does he treat you, Mother ? Does he pester you with shawls for your shoulders to keep the air off, with hats and overshoes and gloves ? Eh, does he ? Does he protect you from draughts and shade you from the sun and hurry you out of the rain ?

MOTHER : Listen, my goodness me ! He asks me that, when he can see for himself how it is. My son pushes me into a cart and bumps and bangs me a million miles until I am the colour of midnight. And then he tips me out on to the hard ground as though I was refuse. And then into the cart I go again and over the hills, with the sun on me and the rain on me, and snow would have been all the same if it had come. But he is a good boy and his singing voice has improved wonderfully on the journey.

TAWM : He's a credit to you, Mother, and I shall borrow him from you when the need arises. We must find him work to do. My son is a good son, too, but he has gone off to the city. He wasn't a ferret either. Here's the farmer coming along that he was shepherd to. He'll be short-handed without my boy. (*To* CUTHMAN.) Can you manage sheep ?

CUTHMAN : I looked after them for my father.

MOTHER : He's a great lover of animals, aren't you, Cuthman ? And, as I say to him, animals know. Even sheep know. He can do anything he likes with them.

[*The* FARMER *comes up to them.*

FARMER : Good-evening, Tawm.

TAWM : You'll be needing another hand, I shouldn't be surprised, now that my son has gone scrimshanking off to the city.

FARMER : It's a loss, Tawm, and a pity he couldn't settle himself down like anyone else. Work's heavy enough at this time of year without being hobbled by a man short.

TAWM : Never in all my years, Mister, have I known a time when young men were scarcer.

FARMER : That's true, Tawm ; there never has been such a time.

TAWM : I've been thinking, Mister ; there's a young man here might do you fine. He's just such a one as my son was. He knows the difference between a man and a piece of flimsy.

FARMER (to CUTHMAN) : Are you a shepherd, son ?

CUTHMAN : Yes, sir ; I was shepherd for my father.

FARMER : Strangers, eh ?

CUTHMAN : Yes, sir ; strangers.

FARMER : Well, you've come at a good time. We can do with you. Is this your mother ?

MOTHER : I'm his mother and there's one thing in the world I need, and that's a cushion at my back. Give me a rest and I shall begin to understand that good fortune's come our way at last.

TAWM : You can think yourself lucky, Mother, that life isn't for ever shoving a footstool under your feet.

FARMER : Come back to my house with me ; we'll talk about this. There's a pot of stew on the fire that I shall be eating for three days if I can't find some one to help me out with it.

DAUGHTER (to TAWM) : Father, come in do. Your supper will be spoiled and you'll be in bed to-morrow with this dew soaking into your feet.

TAWM (to MOTHER) : You see how it is, neighbour ; you see how it is.

MOTHER : It is just like old times to hear you calling me Neighbour ; everything is most delightful.

CUTHMAN : I'll fetch the cart and catch you up.

[*Exeunt Omnes, except* CUTHMAN, *who goes to the cart.*

28

You see what comfort you have brought to us,
Old rough and ready ! But your work's not over.
Those others have already forgotten the church
I've come to build, or find it hard to believe.
But when creation's tide crawled on its first
Advance across the sand of the air, and earth
Tossed its tentative hills, this place of idle
Grass where we are idling took the imprint
Of a dedication, which interminable
History could not weather away. And now
The consummation climbs on to the hill :
A church where the sun will beat on the bell, a church
To hold in its sanctuary the last light.
God be on the hill, and in my heart
And hand. God guide the hammer and the plane.
As the root is guided. Let there be a church.—

[*He grips the handles of the cart.*

Come on now, rough and ready.

[*Exit* CUTHMAN *with the cart.*

[*Enter two brothers,* ALFRED *and* DEMIWULF, *the sons of* MRS.
FIPPS, *who later will give her name to Fippa's Pit : Fippa
Puteus.*

ALFRED : A fat lot of good it is mooching about with a
scowl on your face. It only makes you look like a sick dog.
We must make the place too hot to hold him ; there's
nothing else for it.

DEMIWULF : So we will, so we certainly will ! I'll make sure
he goes off with a flea in his ear !——

ALFRED : Well, let's see you. He's been here a week and
you've done precious little so far, except grind your teeth.

DEMIWULF : That's all you know. I've been speaking to
people about it.

ALFRED : And what good's that, I'd like to know ? What
earthly good is it ? Nobody has any ears for anyone except

this ninny hammer of a boy. There's no sociability in the village any longer, that's what I say. Nobody ever comes to play bowls on Saturday evenings. We can't even put up a shove-ha'penny team against Bramber. Nobody can think of anything except this crazy idea of building a church.

DEMIWULF : They're a lot of gooseheads ; they're a set of nincompoops, all of them, the whole lot of them ! There's not a body in the village that hasn't been bitten by it, except we two and mother.

ALFRED : The farmer has given him the ground.

DEMIWULF : The builder has given him the bricks.

ALFRED : The woodman has given him the timber.

DEMIWULF : Everybody is making a fool of himself in his own way.

ALFRED : Except we two and mother.

DEMIWULF : Let's walk over to Bramber. I'm sick of the whole thing.

[*Exeunt.*

THE PEOPLE OF SOUTH ENGLAND :
  Let time rely on the regular interval
  Of days, but we do no such thing. We pull
  Down the weeks and months like a bough of cherry
  To decorate our room : strip off the year
  As lightly as we tear off the forgotten
  Calendar. But the story must be told.
  We make a country dance of Cuthman's labours
  And widely separated days become near neighbours.

[*Enter* CUTHMAN'S MOTHER *wearing a white apron.*

MOTHER : It's an astonishing thing how time flies. It only seems yesterday that I was being bounced all over the world, and now we've been settled in Steyning for six months as though we had lived here all our lives. Every one has been very kind. Cuthman is earning quite good money from the gentleman we met on the first evening we

30

came. We live in a very nice little cottage. There are rather too many steps but one can't expect everything. Every day I put on a clean apron and the neighbours tell me that they liked the look of me at once. We are already very respected. And it is really wonderful the way everybody helps my son with his church. Every spare moment they have they go with him and do a little more. Besides giving the field, the gentleman we met on the first evening has also given two oxen to help with the work. I told Cuthman that I thought it was extremely generous and he ought to feel very fortunate. When I have finished my work I go down to the church and watch all the villagers singing and hammering in the cool of the day. . . . Well, I must now draw to a close. I have some milk on the fire and by this time it will probably all be boiled over.

[*Exit.*

[*Enter* CUTHMAN, *dragging behind him an oxen-yoke. Enter to him* ALFRED *and* DEMIWULF.

CUTHMAN : Good-afternoon, neighbours.

[*The* BROTHERS *pass by without speaking.*

CUTHMAN : Could you tell me—have you seen my oxen ?

ALFRED (*to* DEMIWULF) : Was the boy speaking to us ?

DEMIWULF : I think he was. Something about oxen.

ALFRED (*to* CUTHMAN) : Are you wanting something ?

CUTHMAN : My two oxen have strayed away somewhere. They're working with us on the church and we're needing them. Have you seen them anywhere about ?

ALFRED : Not a sign. We've seen two oxen belonging to your master.

CUTHMAN : My master gave them to me for the work of the church. Where did you see them ?

DEMIWULF : They were on our land.

ALFRED : Trespassing.

31

DEMIWULF : So we shut them up.

CUTHMAN : I'm sorry they were trespassing. I'll see in future that they stay where they belong. If you could fetch them for me I'll put them to work.

ALFRED : Oh no.

DEMIWULF : Oh no. They stay where they are.

CUTHMAN : We need them.

ALFRED : Then it's a pity you let them go plunging about on other people's property.

DEMIWULF : Where they are they'll stay, and that's flat.

CUTHMAN : What purpose will they serve shut up in a barn ? We need them for the building.

ALFRED : So we heard you say.

CUTHMAN : There's one thing that I'll not see any man destroy ; there's one fire in me that no man shall put out. I am dangerous as I stand over the foundations of the church. I have the unsleeping eyes of a watch-dog.

DEMIWULF : Go and yoke yourself. No doubt you'll find somebody who'll be only too pleased to drive you.

CUTHMAN : I ask you again : Let me have those oxen.

ALFRED : I'm sorry. I'm afraid there's nothing we can do about it.

CUTHMAN : Then I must move. One day I took a crook
And drew a circle in pasture ; and to-day
I draw a circle here to guard the church,
A circle of a stronger faith than I
Could ever have mastered then. Already you slough
Your little spite ; it has deserted you,
And all your power to stir and strength to speak
Has fallen round your ankles, where it hangs
With the weight of chain. And you are naked

Without your fashion of malice, and dumb without
Your surly tongues. But you shall help with the church
Since you refuse the oxen. You shall have
Their glory.

> [*He yokes them together. As he does so the* NEIGHBOURS *enter
> and stand a little way off.*

1ST NEIGHBOUR : Look what Cuthman is doing !

2ND NEIGHBOUR : Look ! He is yoking them !

OTHERS : Can he be joking ? Is this in fun ?
They would never permit. They'd never allow
Liberties for the sake of a laugh.
He is angry. He is driving them
As though they were shallow-skulls,
As though they were thick-skins,
As though they were beasts of the field.

1ST NEIGHBOUR : It is neither anger nor fun.
It is the same stress that we see
Knotting his forearm and kneading his forehead
To drops of sweat when he wrestles
With timber in the framework of the church.

2ND NEIGHBOUR : What will their mother have to say
about it ?

MRS. FIPPS (*bursting through the crowd*) :
I'll show you what their mother will have to say !
What's come over you all to stand and gape,
With outrage running to seed under your eyes ?
Do you want all our days to be choked with insults
And devilment ? We've stood a lot too much
Nonsense from this canting baby,
A lot too much.

(*To* CUTHMAN.) Take that off the backs of my sons and get
out of this place. Do you hear me ? Get out of this place !
Take it off, I tell you ! And don't let me see you or your
amiable mother skulking round these parts any longer.
Do you hear what I say ?

CUTHMAN : Wait a moment. Your sons have shut up the oxen that were helping with the church. I asked them to give them back to us, but that's something they're not prepared to do. The building shall not be interrupted. If they'll not return the oxen they must replace them.

MRS. FIPPS : You overbearing little brat ! You'll be shut up yourself if I have anything to do with it ; I'll see to it ! I'll put you and your mother on the way where you belong —in the ditch with vagrants ! My poor Alfred, my poor Demiwulf, your mother will see that the nasty wicked boy doesn't hurt you. . . . It's your mother talking to you. Alfred ! Demiwulf ! Can't you hear me ?—You've murdered them on their legs, that's what you've done. Take that thing off their backs before I get my hands to you. Go on ! You insolent bantam ! Do what I say ! . . . (*A change comes over her.*) What's happening ? I'm being pushed over ! I'm being knocked down !

NEIGHBOURS : What a wind has got up ! What a gale !

MRS. FIPPS : Help ! Help ! The wind is blowing me over !

NEIGHBOURS : Mind your heads ! The chimneys will be off !

What a tornado !

MRS. FIPPS : Help ! It's whirling me round !
It'll have me off my feet !

NEIGHBOURS : It will have her down !
Look at her, look at her now !

MRS. FIPPS : Help ! Help !

[*The wind blows her out of sight.*

THE PEOPLE OF SOUTH ENGLAND :
The arms of the wood were not ready for this,
The turbulent boy who has pitched himself suddenly in,
The headlong ruffian hurling himself in the lap
Of the valley :
What can protect us from this ragamuffin
Who has stampeded into his manhood with

34

The shudder of the first anger of a rocket ?
He has slammed back the ocean's stable-doors
And slapped the sturdy bases of the earth,
Wrenched and worried into the heart of heaven
And dragged a bellowing Lucifer to ground.
He has belaboured the homeflight of the day
Into a staggered bird. The word's gone round :
There will be no quarter, no pouring of oil.
The roots clutch in the soil, frantic against
The sobbing of the bough. The gates of evening
Clang in vain. Darkness will topple down
Under the guns of the enormous air.
It has lifted an old woman off her feet !
This is a matter of considerable local interest.
It is carrying her up as high as the trees,
Zigzag like a paper bag, like somebody's hat !
There hasn't been a hurricane like this
In living memory. It only shows
How ludicrous it is to strut in a storm.
Zigzag like a paper bag, like somebody's hat !
It will be a long time before we have exhausted
All the possibilities of a story
As amazing as this one is. Up ! Up ! Up !

NEIGHBOURS : Up ! Up ! Up !

[*The* NEIGHBOURS *with shrieks and squeals rush off to follow
the old woman's flight.*

THE PEOPLE OF SOUTH ENGLAND :
You may not think it possible, but tradition
Has it that this old woman was carried five
Miles and dropped in a pond. It's scarcely
Credible, but that is the story that got
About. And when the hurricane had dropped her
It dropped itself and the incident was closed.

CUTHMAN (*unyoking the* BROTHERS) : Well, that was an up-
heaval. You'd better go and look for your mother. She'll
be some way off by this time.

35

ALFRED : I'm not feeling very well. It's as though I was convalescing after a long illness. My voice seems to be climbing back on to my tongue.

DEMIWULF : I feel like a toad crawling out from under a stone.

CUTHMAN : Before you do anything else perhaps you would fetch the oxen for me ? It's time we got busy with them.

ALFRED : We'll fetch them for you at once.

DEMIWULF : At once. We're sorry if you have been put to any inconvenience.

CUTHMAN : The inconvenience was mutual. I shall be at the church.

[*Exit* CUTHMAN.

ALFRED (*as he and his brother go off*) : I wonder where mother is by now ? She always disliked long journeys, but at any rate she hasn't got any luggage to worry about.

THE PEOPLE OF SOUTH ENGLAND :
Do you catch the time of the tune that the shepherd plays
Under the irregular bough of the oak-tree,
The tune of the tale he expects your brain to dance to,
The time of the tune as irregular as the bough ?
It will not come as anything fresh to you
That instead of events keeping their proper stations
They are huddling together as though to find protection
From rain that spoils the mowers' crop
From wind sweeping old women off their feet.
We merely remind you, though we've told you before,
How things stand. We're apt to take the meticulous
Intervention of the sun, the strict
Moon and the seasons much too much for granted.

[*Enter* CUTHMAN'S MOTHER *and* TAWM. *Enter to them some of the* NEIGHBOURS, *downcast.*

MOTHER : I can hardly wait for my son to know. He has

already grown to love you like a father, I know that ; he has often told me so. It is nearly two years since we first met. How astonishing, two years ! Do you remember how we arrived with that dreadful cart ? I was so ashamed. You must have thought we were nothing but riff-raff, and little did I imagine what was in store for us. Usually my intuition is most acute ; things say themselves to me. But oddly enough nothing said to me " One day that dear man is going to be your husband ", nothing at all.—Here are some of the neighbours coming from the church. It's getting on so nicely. Good-evening, neighbours. Is it nearly done ?

1ST NEIGHBOUR : It'll never be done.

2ND NEIGHBOUR : It'll never be finished now.

1ST NEIGHBOUR : There'll be no church.

MOTHER : Never be finished ? Tush and nonsense ! What creatures men are. You're up to the roof.

1ST NEIGHBOUR : Up to the roof we may be but we'll get no farther. The king-post has beaten us.

TAWM : You can't be beaten by a piece of timber ; it isn't princely in a man to be beaten by a piece of timber.

MOTHER : Listen to what he says and be ashamed of yourselves. We are old, this dear man and I, and we know what is right.

1ST NEIGHBOUR : The work was almost done, and then someone suddenly shouted " The king-post has swung out of position ! " It had set other places wrong, that had been ready. For days we have laboured at it, and as time went on we laboured and prayed, but nothing will make it go into its place. We're not knowledgeable men with these things. It's not our work and a church isn't like a little cottage. We've none of the proper appurtenances for the job. There's no hope for it, even if we go on trying till we're whiteheaded.

MOTHER : But Cuthman—he thinks of nothing but how the

building grows, nothing but of the day when it will be done
—where is he? What is he doing?

2ND NEIGHBOUR : We couldn't get him away. For days he
has tugged and tusselled with us, with the blood in his face
and the veins pushing in his head. And now he has gone
into a ghost. He smoothes the stone with his hand as though
it were in a fever and sleepless. He pats it as though it were
a horse that had brought him safely through battle. And
then he stands heavily in the aisle with his misery staring
to the east.

MOTHER : Poor Cuthman, poor sweet son ! On our journey
it was ahead of him like riches, and every moment of his
holiday time he has run to it as though he had heaven at
his shoulders. This will damage him. I'm afraid for him
and I don't mind telling you.

TAWM : Here's the boy ; here he is.

[*Enter* CUTHMAN *running. Other* NEIGHBOURS *join the group.*

MOTHER : Cuthman, what has happened to you? Son,
What is the matter ?

CUTHMAN :   The king-post is in place
Again ! The church will be finished.

MOTHER :   But the neighbours
Said there was no one with you. You were alone.

CUTHMAN : I was alone by the unattended pillar,
 Mourning the bereaved air that lay so quiet
 Between walls ; hungry for hammer-blows
 And the momentous hive that once was there.
 And when I prayed my voice slid to the ground
 Like a crashed pediment.
 There was a demolition written over
 The walls, and dogs rummaged in the foundations,
 And picnic parties laughed on a heap of stone.
 But gradually I was aware of some one in
 The doorway and turned my eyes that way and saw

38

Carved out of the sunlight a man who stood
Watching me, so still that there was not
Other such stillness anywhere on the earth,
So still that the air seemed to leap
At his side. He came towards me, and the sun
Flooded its banks and flowed across the shadow.
He asked me why I stood alone. His voice
Hovered on memory with open wings
And drew itself up from a chine of silence
As though it had longtime lain in a vein of gold.
I told him : It is the king-post.
He stretched his hand upon it. At his touch
It lifted to its place. There was no sound.
I cried out, and I cried at last " Who are you ? "
I heard him say " I was a carpenter " . . .

   [They fall upon their knees.

There under the bare walls of our labour
Death and life were knotted in one strength
Indivisible as root and sky.

THE PEOPLE OF SOUTH ENGLAND :
The candle of our story has burnt down
And Cuthman's life is puffed like a dandelion
Into uncertain places. But the hand
Still leads the earth to drink at the sky, and still
The messenger rides into the city of leaves
Under the gradual fires of September ;
The Spring shall hear, the Winter shall be wise
To warning of aconite and freezing lily,
And all shall watch the augur of a star
And learn their stillness from a stiller heaven.

And what of us who upon Cuthman's world
Have grafted progress without lock or ratchet ?
What of us who have to catch up, always
To catch up with the high-powered car, or with
The unbalanced budget, to cope with competition,
To weather the sudden thunder of the uneasy

Frontier ? We also loom with the earth
Over the waterways of space. Between
Our birth and death we may touch understanding
As a moth brushes a window with its wing.

Who shall question then
Why we lean our bicycle against a hedge
And go into the house of God ?
Who shall question
That coming out from our doorways
We have discerned a little, we have known
More than the gossip that comes to us over our gates.